This Handwriting Notebook Belongs To:

A

A is For

B

B is For

C is For

D is For

E is For

F is For

G

G is For

H

H is For

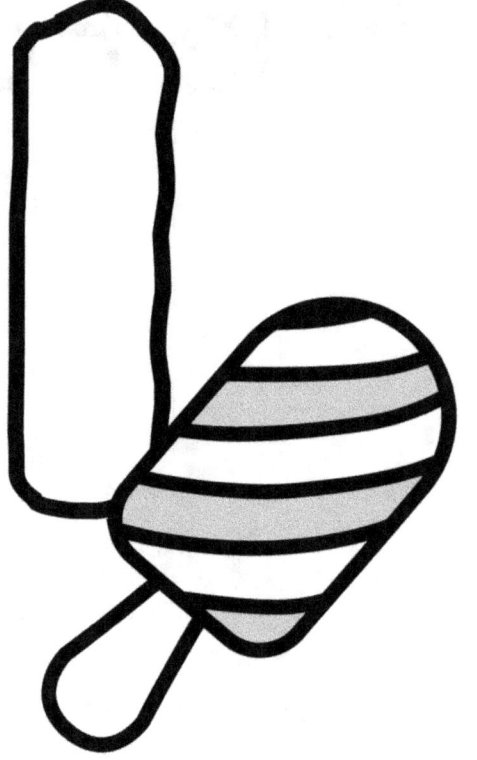

I

I is For

J is For

K is For

L is For

M

M is For

N is For

o

O is For

P

P is For

Q is For

R

R is For

s

S is For

T

T is For

U is For

V is For

W

W is For

X is For

Y

Y is For

Z

Z is For

A Is For Angle

B Is For Bless

C Is For Cute

D Is For Do

E Is For Enjoy

F Is For First

G Is For Good

H Is For Heaven

I Is For Idea

J Is For Joy

K Is For Kind

L Is For Life

M Is For Make

N Is For Nice

O Is For Open

P Is For Polite

Q Is For Quiet

R Is For Right

S Is For Super

T Is For Tidy

U Is For Understand

V Is For Value

W Is For Warm

X Is For XXL

Y Is For Youth

Z Is For Zest